On the Appearance of the World

Forerunners: Ideas First

Short books of thought-in-process scholarship, where intense analysis, questioning, and speculation take the lead

FROM THE UNIVERSITY OF MINNESOTA PRESS

(Continued on page 71)

On the Appearance of the World
A Future for Aesthetics in Architecture

Mark Foster Gage

University of Minnesota Press

MINNEAPOLIS
LONDON

Portions of the chapter "The Appearance of Aesthetics" were published in a different form in the Introduction to *Aesthetics Equals Politics: New Discourses across Art, Architecture, and Philosophy,* ed. Mark Foster Gage, 1–23 (Cambridge, Mass.: MIT Press, 2023).

ISBN 978-1-5179-1728-9 (PB)
ISBN 978-1-4529-7114-8 (Ebook)
ISBN 978-1-4529-7185-8 (Manifold)

Published by the University of Minnesota Press, 2024
111 Third Avenue South, Suite 290
Minneapolis, MN 55401-2520
www.upress.umn.edu

Available as a Manifold edition at manifold.umn.edu

The University of Minnesota is an equal-opportunity educator and employer.

Contents

Preface

I MENTALLY MAPPED OUT THIS BOOK during the contemplative solitude that naturally accompanies coast-to-coast motorcycle rides—in my particular case from San Francisco to New York City on a 1200cc Triumph Bonneville. Of course, one should not ride such distances, as motorcycles are rather dangerous (so don't take this as an endorsement for mixing scholarship and easy riding). However, accompanying this danger is also unfiltered and overwhelming access to the appearances of the world around you. Motorcycles have no windshields, dashboards, screens, or roofs, meaning one's field of vision is vastly increased. It was likely this Brobdingnagian perspective that brought to the foreground of my attention the appalling ugliness of the built environment, or put another way, the appalling contemporary environments in which human life takes place today and how they are developed almost entirely without any knowledge of the field of aesthetics.

Somewhere around Utah it became obvious to me that most of the constructed world between San Francisco and New York has been the product of only twentieth-century architectural practices and urban theories. There are no Parises, Kyotos, Sydneys, or Romes between the American coasts. Instead, we have places like Modesto, Reno, Omaha, and Des Moines—all almost entirely dominated by the urbanism of modern-ish office boxes clad in featureless glass, beige stucco strip malls, endless parking lots, and even more endless (if such a thing is possible) suburban sprawl. While entirely unprovable, it takes no particular genius to connect the dots between aesthetics being removed as a subject from architectural education in the years surrounding World War I and a subsequent century of fantastically ugly and inhumane built environments produced by architects almost completely ignorant of aesthetics as a discourse.

And so, upon my iron horse I decided what the world needed most wasn't more deeply jargoned scholarship or indecipherable journal submissions about how terrible the world is—but rather a primer that was more easily consumed. The Forerunners series, with its focus on "Short books of thought-in-process scholarship, where intense analysis, questioning, and speculation take the lead," was the perfect outlet for these developing ideas. On that note, these are very much ideas-in-development, but I thought them worth getting out into the world sooner rather than later in the hope of better articulating how architecture and aesthetics do and can intersect at our particular moment in time to—fingers crossed—help in some small way to point us toward a more beautiful and just century of environment building that we should all hope is forthcoming.

The Appearance of Architecture

IN THE PANTHEON OF GREEK ANTIQUITY, architecture came first. The eldest of the primordial deities to emerge from the spinning cauldron of chaos was Gaia, or Earth, who in the great religious tradition of virgin births herself bore two fatherless sons—being Pontus, the sea, and Ouranoss, the sky. Today we call Ouranoss "Uranus," ironically now meaning not our own sky but rather the seventh planet from our sun—one that isn't even a sky-like gas giant at all but rather a mere ice-giant doppelganger. It's important to note the genealogical calculus surrounding Ouranoss, who came into existence far before the more commonly known standard-issue Greek gods that we know today, and even before their predecessors, the Titans. In this, the sky (Ouranoss) thus precedes both time and beauty, the former his son, Kronos (Time), and the latter his daughter, Aphrodite (Beauty),—who herself was birthed from the foamy mess of Ouranoss's castration at Kronos's gelding hands, which is altogether another story.

Eventually, upon the mating of Kronos with his own sister, Rhea (Earth), we get something starting to resemble architecture—a daughter. She was known as Hestia, goddess of the hearth, being not only fire but the *architecture* that contained it. Unknown to most, Hestia was actually born *first* of all the

Greek gods—as the oldest sibling of Demeter, Poseidon, Hera, and eventually the youngest child, Zeus. Today we know this genealogy in reverse order—Zeus, Hera, Poseidon, Demeter, and poor forgotten Hestia—not because that was the order of their birth but rather for the order in which they were regurgitated by their father, Kronos, after he ate them immediately following their births. That is to say, without culinary infanticide of Kronos, along with Aphrodite, Hestia, goddess of architecture, would have been the first among the gods. That is to say that, were it not for Time, Architecture and Beauty would have, as the two eldest siblings, ruled the world.

This already tricky family genealogy is made even less comprehensible by three millennia of additional confusion, and yet there seems to be a consensus today that architecture has something to do with beauty, and something to do with time—but the linkages, confusing as they were from the very start, have been mostly lost to both time (again), and accordingly, contemporary interest. To further confuse issues, we are no longer allowed to discuss *beauty* in contemporary academic parlance, and instead typically use the distant and more sanitized term *aesthetics,* a word with so many meanings across culture as to be nearly meaningless. All of this requires some clarification.

The Appearance of Aesthetics

IT IS A MERE MORTAL GREEK, Aristotle, who in *De Anima* describes of receiving into oneself, via human senses, the forms that produce our very definition of the world, or rather, our reality. While the term *aesthetics* was introduced only much later in the eighteenth-century work of Alexander Gottlieb Baumgartner and greatly expanded by Immanuel Kant (both German mortals), the idea of a discourse predicated on relationships between humanity and the forms of its reality has appeared in the work of countless thinkers and in a vast array of disciplines over the past two millennia. In this journey—through the hands of not only philosophers A to Z, perhaps Aristotle to Žižek, but also artists, curators, musicians, and critics too many to name—aesthetics has come into contemporary use with a definition that covers an immense intellectual territory.

At least two extreme poles can be identified that define the vast gradient of usage for the term *aesthetics* as it is understood today. The first exists largely as a theoretical heirloom from the late nineteenth century, gifted by the figureheads of the aesthetic movement: Oxford Don Walter Pater and his protégée Oscar Wilde. Within this movement, *aesthetics,* interlaced with the beauty and the arts, was separated from commercial life by being positioned as an *autonomous* human pursuit, a goal to be

3

sought with no concerns for profit, political gain, power, or other polluting aspects of either human greed or commercial exchange. This is generally known as *aesthetic hedonism,* a label with nefarious connotations but that was actually designed to *save* the arts from the destructive capacities of capitalism. Wilde's adage "all art is quite useless" was not intended to demean the value of art culturally but rather to eliminate the value of art *commercially,* as a thing that is useless can only exist outside of the marketplace of financial consumption. Here aesthetic concerns were positioned to be independent from any form of social or political engagement yet maintained a high degree of cultural significance—precisely due to this capitalistic indigestibility.

Many historic and contemporary critiques of aesthetics and claims of cultural anesthetization emerge from variations of this position—namely that aesthetic qualities only form the "useless" separate or illusory, typically subjective, surfaces of appearance that hover above deeper epistemological or political realities of existence. Holding such beliefs almost requires, intellectually, the revealing of such obscured realities that exist underneath these obfuscations—and can be seen championed in the work of past and current philosophers currently including, notably, Slavoj Žižek, through his work on ideology, and Alain Badiou, through his work on the "inaesthetic" and truth procedures. While the exact trajectories of these aesthetic critiques are beyond the ambitions of this text, they are significant for helping define the current status of aesthetics as something primarily, well, useless and superficial.

Instead of being divorced from commerce and politics entirely, as Wilde proposes, my use of the term *aesthetics* in this book lies between this restricted definition and a vastly more encompassing position most forcefully articulated today by philosopher Jacques Rancière, who considers the term to be non–art specific and recasts it what he calls the *Distribution of the Sensible.* In this latter, more encompassing framework, aesthetics defines the relations between the sensible aspects of individual, community, physical, and social life, and accordingly must be a basis for human activity not only in artistic but in political and social registers. In a public dialogue I had with Jacques Rancière at Yale University in 2016, he articulated this contemporary expansion of aesthetics beyond only pertaining to art, as follows:

> For me, aesthetics is not the theory of art, and appreciation of art, or so on. My understanding of aesthetics is twofold. First, the ground meaning of the aesthetic is not about art but what constitutes the sensible experience . . . It is about the experience of a common world and who is able to share this experience. For me politics is aesthetic and, in a sense, it was constituted as such before art.

Later in our conversation he elaborated further on the recasting of aesthetics as the "distribution of the sensible":

> What the idea of the distribution of the sensible implies is that an art always does something else than its proper business. At this point it may meet the paths of emancipation, since emancipation means that you stop doing just your "own business." The aesthetic is not the same as the artistic. The artistic is about the implementation of an idea. It implies some kind of anticipation of the result, which may be put to the extreme in the case of political art. Instead, the aesthetic means that you don't exactly know what will be the effect of what you are doing.

While it is a burgeoning twenty-first-century cliché to assume all academic endeavors are the proper vehicles for social and political engagement, it is the case that the aesthetic has a particularly strong claim to such relevance through the combination of the above relationships through which political relations are now beginning to be understood. While these concerns are often spoken of as problems of policy in the political sciences and sociology, they are rarely addressed as problems of aesthetic practices. This book is an act of speculation regarding how a reignited discourse of the aesthetic and the extended, but not limitless, spaces of its understood influence can prompt new relations between not only objects, spaces, environments, and ecologies, but also with each other and the *visible structures in which we are all enmeshed*—that is to say, the appearance of the world.

Given the vast and explosive interest in aesthetics in multiple fields today, this, I hope, will help prompt what has been elsewhere referred to as one of an ongoing series of philosophical "turns"—an "Aesthetic Turn," as the case may be, that includes a wide array of vibrant new discourses in multiple disciplines. To adopt such a name is intentionally referential, and perhaps overturns the original developments of the "Linguistic Turn," the name coined from the collected essays of Richard Rorty in 1967. While the Linguistic Turn referred to the perceived idealism-derived dominance of language in defining reality, such sentiments were far earlier articulated by the prescient Wittgenstein in his *Tractatus Logicio-Philosophicus* as "the limits of my language are the limits of my world" (1921), or Derrida's "there is nothing outside the text" (*Of Grammatology,* 1967). As such, the Aesthetic Turn might revise, perhaps ironically, the languages of the Linguistic Turn in order to propose yet another inversion, where: "The limits of my aesthetic perception are the limits of my world," or "everything is outside the text." An Aesthetic Turn would not be a new theory but rather a new intellectual foundation on which new theories for multiple disciplines might be constructed. Here we are concerned with how this expanded *but neither useless nor limitless* idea of aesthetics might begin to operate in the emerging architectural discourses and professions of the twenty-first century.

Architecture as an Art/Not-Art

SO WHAT EXACTLY is the current relationship between aesthetics and architecture? Those in either field would likely be surprised to find that there is not much of one, at least not connecting any of the contemporary worlds of architectural theory, architectural education, architectural practice, and aesthetic philosophy.[1] Why is architecture so rarely considered worthy of aesthetic attention within philosophy?[2] Or why is the field of aesthetics not worthy of the attention of architects or architectural theorists? Perhaps it

1. There are few published exceptions to this claim, and those exceptions have garnered very little attention within the field of architectural theory. I refer to books including: Roger Scruton's *The Aesthetics of Architecture* (1979), Richard Hill's *Designs and Their Consequences: Architecture and Aesthetics* (1999), and Allen Carlson's *Aesthetics and the Environment: Art and Architecture* (2000). My own books linking aesthetics with architecture are perhaps too recent to claim any sort of success or failure on this front and include: *Aesthetic Theory: Essential Texts* (2011), *Aesthetics Equals Politics: New Discourses across Art, Architecture, and Philosophy* (2018), and *Designing Social Equality: Architecture, Aesthetics and the Perception of Democracy* (2019).

2. There are authors who have addressed the subject of architectural aesthetics, but they are very limited, including figures such as Roger Scruton and Branko Mitrovic. The point being that while architects make aesthetic decisions, there is no discourse of aesthetics withing architectural practice or education.

would be a natural starting point to ask if architecture is deserving of aesthetic consideration at all. Aesthetics has until recently, as defined by Wilde and Pater, been a discourse reserved for the arts, and within those arts attention has been directed nearly exclusively toward painting and sculpture, with photography and music in very distant third and fourth places, respectively. Largely missing from this equation—and despite the time- and beauty-entwined circumstances of her birth—has been architecture. In order to recalibrate these relations, I believe there needs to be a precise, surgical procedure that gently decouples aesthetics from pertaining only to the "arts," toward a *qualified, not all-inclusive,* "distribution of the sensible," as articulated by Rancière. It is in this interstitial territory that the future value of aesthetic discourse for architecture will be shown to exist.

The Separation of Art, Architecture, and Aesthetics

ALTHOUGH ARCHITECTURE has historically been considered a "fine art," oftentimes standing alongside painting, sculpture, music, and poetry, its status as an equal has always been in question. This unequal status emerges from the burden of architecture's defining requirement to *function*—a trait not equally shared by other artforms. Architecture's qualifications for aesthetic attention have been frequently in question because of this need to function, or its corollary: that it is *not* produced exclusively for artistic pleasure or contemplation.[1] Confusion, however, emerges in that, while architecture is not produced *exclusively* for artistic enjoyment, it is at times enjoyed for its artistic qualities, meaning

1. I once had the pleasure of coteaching a graduate design studio at Yale University with the architect Frank Gehry. For the final review we invited the celebrated sculptor Richard Serra to Yale to discuss the work of the students and ideas prompted by the course. A friendly argument ensued between Frank and Richard regarding how one could reasonably distinguish sculpture from architecture in definitive terms. Serra offered the defining trait of plumbing. If it had plumbing it was not sculpture but architecture. The debate continues.

that, while its claim to artistic status is not as stable as that of painting or sculpture, it does reasonably exist.

One logical direction to pursue further, if one sought to ensure aesthetic attention for architecture, would be to better confirm this status as an art—as if, were it more surefooted in such status, it would be more likely to be confirmed as deserving of aesthetic attention both within and outside of the field. Architects have sought such artistic status for architecture at least since the early Renaissance, an early effort that is conveyed notably by the title of the first book on architecture theory, Leon Battista Alberti's 1452 *On the Art of Building in Ten Books (De Re Aedificatoria)*. This is further evinced in Georgio Vasari's mid-Renaissance publication that arrived nearly a century later in 1568, titled *The Lives of the Most Excellent Painters, Sculptors, and Architects (Le Vite de' Più Eccellenti Pittori, Scultori, e Architettori)*, which again, as is obvious in the title, attempts to elevate architects from their previous status as mere craftsmen to the higher status of "artist" alongside those of painters and sculptors.

The ensuing long-term struggle between architecture being an art or not-art, however, will not be a battle fought yet again in this book. Instead, I propose that while architecture's legitimacy for aesthetic attention could be partially verified by its status as an art, it has a greater claim by virtue of its increasingly dominant role in *establishing the visual framework of human perception*. I will also propose that this increasing impact of architecture on the human field of vision warrants a broadening of aesthetic discourse, such that aesthetic discourse can be stretched to include nonart cultural entities, yet not be tasked with accommodating *all* entities, as is the case with a Rancierian position.

The weakness of trying to confirm architecture's status as an art in order to justify it for aesthetic attention requires some consideration. The status of what does and does not fall into the category of "art" has been and continues to be a subject fraught with centuries of controversy and continues into the recent history of analytic philosophy. An early attempt at defining art in the analytic tradition can be found in the Wittgenstein-based definition offered by Morris Weitz, who in 1956 argued that, in fact, no definition of art is possible because art is an "open concept," and any static definition would therefore "compromise the creativity" of art. Weitz writes "To understand the role of aesthetic theory is not to conceive of it as a definition, logically doomed to failure," meaning that the role of aesthetics is not to define what is art or not art, but rather, as he continues, "to attend in certain ways to features of art."[2] Within this definition (or nondefinition, rather), architecture could not be denied status as an art, and would therefore be worthy of aesthetic attention—but only alongside *everything else in the world*. It follows that if everything can be considered art, then the distinction of what is and what is not art becomes meaningless. Similarly, if *everything* is deserving of aesthetic attention, the nothing *in particular* is deserving of aesthetic attention.

A different strategy for artistic categorization lies the 1983 definition offered by George Dickie, who claimed that a work of art should be defined as "an artifact of a kind created to be presented to an artworld public," which would *disqualify* architecture for status as an art, as architecture is created for a public larger than only an artworld public.[3] More recently Yuriko Saito, in her book *Everyday Aesthetics* sought to bypass the art question entirely and claimed that confining aesthetics to art undermines percipients' ability to engage with aesthetic properties of objects in everyday reality, a position that would, again *reinstate* archi-

2. Weitz, "The Role of Theory in Aesthetics," 27.
3. Dickie, "The New Institutional Theory of Art," 57–64.

tecture as worthy of aesthetic consideration but, again, only by virtue of its everydayness rather than its artistic value.[4] (This is an expansion of aesthetic reach within analytic philosophy and loosely mirrors Rancière's similar expansion, albeit for different reasons, within Continental philosophy.) Saito's position would contradict Dickie's 1983 definition and return us to a descendant position of Weitz's 1956 definition, notably that aesthetics should not be confined to art, and that architecture would be worthy of aesthetic consideration—but again, only alongside everything else in the world. For our purposes, a final foray into the debate regarding the position of architecture as an art relative to aesthetics can be found in James Shelley's 2018 paper "The Default Theory of Aesthetic Value," where he describes that "works of literature are aesthetic objects as surely and as fully as are paintings, sculptures, musical pieces and dances"— yet with no mention of architecture.[5] Thus, architecture would once again be *disqualified* from warranting aesthetic attention, by Shelley's precise omission.

As is apparent, the problem with seeking to define architecture as an art in order to qualify it for aesthetic consideration is that even after centuries of debate there appears to be no impending resolution to the question, whether it be within art, architecture, art history, architectural theory, or aesthetic philosophy. Nonetheless, the world must go on and architecture must be built—only without any resolution of its artistic status or, I would argue, the much more important associated status of being considered worthy of *aesthetic attention* and guidance that comes with legitimized status as an art.

4. Saito, *Everyday Aesthetics*.
5. James Shelley, "The Default Theory of Aesthetic Value," 3.

Architecture's aesthetic dilemma is that it is currently stretched between two dominant positions with which to consider its value for aesthetic attention, being:

1. Architecture *is* an art, and therefore is deserving of aesthetic attention, or
2. Because art cannot be defined or should not be considered a special category, *everything* is deserving of aesthetic consideration.

While such indeterminate theoretical stretching may be serviceable for other arts (or nonarts), such an extreme taffying is particularly damaging to architecture as it places architecture in a perpetual state where it remains simultaneously not quite enough of an art to be an art, yet by most accounts is too special to be a mere everyday thing.[6] By existing in this categorical limbo architecture receives not only no philosophical attention but also troublingly little *aesthetic* attention, as if there was going to be a gateway for philosophical attention for architecture, it would likely be through aesthetics. One might worry that neither philosophy nor aesthetics have any meaningful relationship with architectural theory, discourse, or education, despite architecture being the physically largest and most resource consuming of all human endeavors. Such worry would seem warranted.

Participating in the tennis match of architecture's artistic and therefore aesthetic value therefore seems to be a fruitless endeavor, continually leaving architecture without any accompanying aesthetic discourse to guide or inform its creative production. I, therefore, suggest that we forgo the question of art and work in reverse, shifting from aesthetics back into architecture via

6. Such as Saito's example of laundry being deserving of aesthetic attention. Saito, "The Aesthetics of Laundry" in *Aesthetics of the Familiar,* 115.

another route of legitimization. Architecture's qualification for aesthetic consideration, therefore, would need to come from a location *other* than its status as being, or not being, an art.

I suggest that aesthetic discourse could be slightly broadened to accommodate not only historically verifiable "art," but also entities that are *special enough* through *cultural* characteristics other than only full artistic status, yet in doing so it not be broadened so widely as to include all entities, everywhere, and always, as is suggested within the Continental tradition by Rancière and, in the analytic tradition by Saito. To proceed with further arguments, I will therefore assume as most reasonable what I have termed a *limited aesthetic expansion,* where it would include architecture *if* architecture were able to be, if not a fully recognized art, then at least more valuable to human culture than all everyday objects, everywhere. I would also suggest that the nonart cultural value of architecture, today more than ever before, will emerge from its newly minted status as the visual framework of human perception.[7]

7. This particular insight and framing was presented by architectural theorist David Ruy during a public lecture titled: "Returning to (Strange) Objects."

Architecture as the Framework of Human Perception

Aesthetics have substantial political consequences. How one views oneself . . . has deep consequences in terms of one's feelings of self-worth and one's capacity to be a political agent.

—CORNEL WEST, *Breaking Bread: Insurgent Black Intellectual Life*

IN 2016 the United Nations Department of Economic and Social Affairs published a report that went surprisingly unnoticed— which declared that for first time in human history more of the global population now lived in cities than in rural areas.[1] This event, happening in the lifetime of any readers of these words is rather extraordinary, but especially for architects, as it means that when the majority of humankind (at the time of writing 54 percent to be exact) exits the front door of their home or building of residence, their visual field is defined not by a natural ecologi-

1. Population information retrieved from the "2014 Revision of World Urbanization Prospects," produced by the *Population Division of the UN Department of Economic and Social Affairs (UN DESA)*. https:// www.un.org/en/development/desa/publications/2014-revision-world -urbanization-prospects.html.

cal horizon but an architectural one—in the form of cities. If one were to extrapolate further it could be reasonably claimed that architecture has thus had a shift in its historical role from being the discipline responsible for producing the enclosures that protect humans from nature, to a contemporary position as the discipline responsible for producing the majority of the visual framework of human perception.[2] This realignment within the field of architecture warrants significant further consideration in multiple disciplines, yet for the purpose of this essay it is enough to allow me to make my claim—that independent of its status as an art or nonart, the shift in architecture status qualifies it to be of *enough* cultural significance that it requires consideration in aesthetic registers in philosophy as well as in architectural theory and practice.[3]

While it may seem unusual to contemporary readers to be presented with such a strong link between the discipline of architecture and the perception of human reality, architecture, in fact, has a long history of calibrating the human perception of reality, albeit in more focused registers. While the full extent of these relationships is beyond the ambitions of our subject, it may be useful to note a few examples that anticipate architecture's

2. In Act II of Shakespeare's *As You Like It,* the nobleman Jacques, exiled to the Forest of Arden, speaks the infamous words "All the worlds a stage," which has perhaps been realized to an extent that would likely surprise the Bard himself.

3. It may be that this increased role for architecture withing the human visual field would also meet Morris Weitz's and Yuriko Saito's more open definitions of what warrants aesthetic attention, and possibly address George Dickie's qualifier that art be for an artworld audience, in that all of the "artworld public" exist in the general public that would be exposed to architecture. Only James Shelley's formalist definition requiring precisely and only the production of pleasure in defining aesthetic value would continue to resist the inclusion of architecture as warranting aesthetic attention.

role in defining the visual framework of human perception.[4] For instance, on the Athenian Acropolis lies the infamous Parthenon, completed in 438 BCE, which included in its construction exquisite and purposeful mutations of the rigid systems of classical architecture that were designed to overcome what were perceived faults in human visual perception. These were known as *optical refinements* and were introduced into the design of the Parthenon, at staggering expense, to recalibrate how the human eye perceives the visual reality of the building to appear more optically perfect. As the temples of Greek antiquity became larger, the perspectival distortions became greater. Their response was to introduce these shape anomalies that torque, twist, tilt, bend, and skew architectural elements so that while they disobeyed the strict rules of classical architecture, they *appeared* to better follow them.

We find another example of architecture being asked to revise the visual framework of human perception nearly five hundred years after the previous example, this time in Roman antiquity—through the writings of Roman architect and engineer Marcus Vitruvius Pollio. In Book VI, Chapter II of his *Ten Books on Architecture* he writes, "If things that are true appear false, there should be no doubt that it is proper to make additions and subtractions according to the nature of the site."[5] Here he is indicating, once again, that it is the responsibility of the architect not only to construct buildings but to orchestrate their visual perception through unorthodox adjustments to their physical form.

A final example, among many possible, occurs in the nascent Florentine Renaissance, nearly 1500 years after the writings of Vitruvius, where in 1421 architect Filippo Brunelleschi con-

4. A note that, because of my own limited background, these are all Western examples, and further examination would likely reveal other such instances in other cultures.

5. Vitrivius, *Ten Books on Architecture*, 6.2.

ducted his legendary "perspectival experiments" in front of the Florentine Baptistery, adjacent to the Duomo where he was employed as the master architect for the construction of the then incomplete dome. Through using mirrors, drawings, and sightlines, Brunelleschi discovered how to accurately calculate horizon line isocephaly, the form of perspective drawing that allows one to calculate perceived distance away from the human eye using a third dimension, being representational depth. Perspective drawing was, for architecture, a tool used as an accurate *predictor of the visual appearance of reality* prior to its actual construction, thereby enabling new trajectories in not only architectural design, where the technique originated, but also in painting, the combination of which we would later recognize as the Italian Renaissance.

At this point we will accept that architecture's status as an art or nonart is, for the time being, unresolvable, and that in lieu of such resolution, the contemporary claim for aesthetic consideration within architecture emerges from its recent transition from producing objects in a field of "nature" to defining the majority of the visual framework of human perception—a continuation of the line of inquiry inaugurated in the Renaissance, and therefore hardly a newcomer to the discipline.[6] The question, then, would be that while architecture is *qualified* to be a subject for aesthetic consideration, does the discipline of architecture, via architects, *want* to engage in such discourse? The answer for the past century and up through the current moment has been a resounding no. Why is this so?

6. Such a position could also hold that architecture, while perhaps not one of the "official" fine arts, is *enough* of an art, and that this status combined with its increasing role in defining the visual framework of reality qualify it for *some* relationship with the field of aesthetics, the extent of which remains to be determined.

Architecture's Aesthetic Allergy

ARCHITECTURE'S LACK of a relationship to aesthetic philosophy today is a product of the belief that, in the most positive case, aesthetic concerns in architecture are merely superficial compared to the more important subjects of function, and, in the most negative case, that aesthetic considerations in architecture are nefariously abused by those in power to obscure truths they wish to remain hidden. The first critique is perhaps nowhere more visible than in the (warning: offensive) words of one of architectural modernism's key founders, Le Corbusier, who in 1927 stated regarding aesthetic concerns that they were "of a sensorial and elementary order [. . .] suited to simple races, peasants and savages."[1] Le Corbusier's socially appalling but also aesthetically suppressive belief was that the aesthetic qualities of physical material were *base concerns* and needed to be replaced

1. I find it difficult to include these words here for publication but decided to do so in order to convey the vitriolic disdain felt for aesthetic concerns within early Architectural Modernism. It is worth noting that Architectural Modernism as a movement supposedly had high moral aspirations toward equality—although these are hardly conveyed by Le Corbusier's sentiments. See Le Corbusier, *Towards a New Architecture*, 143.

by the "rational contemplation of form."[2] This hard anti-aesthetic position was further calcified into architecture by the subsequent adoption of Marxist critical theory as it was developed by members of the Frankfurt School in interwar Europe and folded into architectural theory in the decades that followed. This would later come to be called the "Critical Project" in architecture. While I have written about the adoption of these ideas and their anti-aesthetic implications for architecture in greater detail elsewhere, what is important to note here is that the primary ambition of the Critical Project within architecture was to reveal the underlying, and often unseen, political, social, and economic power structures that govern the societies in which we live, and to introduce, in the words of David Macey, "a form of self-consciousness that can act as a guide to emancipatory action."[3] Aesthetic ambitions ran counter to these goals as they were seen to merely further obscure unseen power structures, and therefore suppress the self-consciousness that was required for action.

For the descendant discipline of architecture today, aesthetic considerations in both professional and theoretical circles continue to be dismissed as an unimportant superficial layer of appearance that obscures the "real" aspects of architecture that should be more seriously engaged. This perspective is perhaps nowhere more visible than in the 2000 Venice Architecture Biennale curated by the star Italian architect Massimiliano Fuksas, titled "Less Aesthetics, More Ethics."[4] Such an anti-

2. Corbusier, 144.

3. Macey, *The Penguin Dictionary of Critical Theory*, 76.

4. The 2000 Venice Biennale was curated, and so named, by Italian architect Massimiliano Fuksas. Documentation of the Biennale can be found in the accompanying book: Massimiliano Fuksas, *Less Aesthetics More Ethics: The 7th International Venice Architectural Biennale.*

aesthetic position is a difficult territory for architecture to exist within.[5] In a contemporary moment of reflection, we might
now begin to realize that decades of not only nonaesthetic, but
anti-aesthetic theory that have governed the discipline of architecture may have had the result that, among other consequences, a vast rift now separates how architects and designers
discuss and legitimize their work relative to how society receives, understands, and values it—which I suggest is primarily
aesthetically.[6]

Instead of engaging the subject of aesthetics in either architectural theory and practice, architects today tend to em-
ploy abstract "concepts" to justify their production, whether
through the familiar use of architectural symbols, signs, and
indexes, or other "scientism-based" criteria such as sustainability. (What is your "concept" is the typical refrain heard ad
nauseum in architectural juries the world over.) The public at
large, however, judges architecture *aesthetically* and does so
significantly without the knowledge to interpret such works in
terms of their concept, signifying value or ability to function in
particular ways that are described by architects. This disjunc-
tion between how architects produce architecture, devoid of
aesthetic concerns, and how users experience and understand
architecture, aesthetically, has generated decades of architecture of questionable cultural value and service—a situation
that has been noticed by numerous observers. For instance,
architect Steven Bingler and editor Martin C. Pedersen, noted
as much in the *New York Times,* saying that the profession of

5. This is particularly the case as the discipline of architecture is required to deal with the aesthetic concerns of form, color, materials, light,
and texture at a greater scale than nearly any other artistic endeavor.

6. I have found no empirical studies within sociology regarding
this, but certainly they would be warranted.

architecture "has flatly dismissed the general public's take on our work."[7] This is perhaps not a life-threatening situation, but these sentiments herald an ever-widening divide between an architecture that is developed without aesthetic discourse, and a population that judges architecture aesthetically.

7. Martin Pedersen, and Steven Bingler, "How to Rebuild Architecture." *New York Times,* December 14, 2014, Opinion section.

Architecture's Aesthetic Categories

THE VIEW that I have been presenting suggests that a productive shift needs to occur that would move architecture away from the historic anti-aesthetic discourses of functional, modernist, or neo-Marxist critique to those of aesthetics. If we accept that architecture would benefit from a more direct engagement with aesthetics, and therefore visual appearances, the next step would be to assess the aesthetic positions available for architecture, whether in education, theory, or practice.[1] While not claiming to

1. A useful format for this exercise that I adopted can be found in the article "Artistic Style and the Expression of Ideals," by Robert Hopkins and Nick Riggle. Hopkins and Riggle suggest that the distinction between "general" style and "individual" style in the work of artists is significant, as it is through the latter that the artist reveals her driving intent. The categories of such artistic intent are divided into Personality (P), Implied Personality (IP), Artistic Personality (AP), or Artistic Ideals (AI). The conclusion for this article is that, as the title suggests, individual artistic style is best justified as an expression of ideals (AI), largely on ethical grounds. While a full excursus of this article is beyond the boundaries of the architectural and aesthetic question before us, its organization is valuable for assessing similarly defined aesthetic categories, as they anticipate future relationships between architecture and aesthetic discourse, particularly with regard to designers' or artists' intent and, by extension, virtue aesthetics.

be a definitive list, my intent in outlining the following positions is to help form a more clearly defined set of possible positions between architecture and aesthetics, as follows: Anti-Aesthetic (AA), Suppressed Aesthetic (SU), Communicatory Aesthetic (CA), Formalist Aesthetic (FA), and Speculative Aesthetic (SA). Here are my working definitions for each category, all of which receive in-depth descriptions in the following chapters:

ANTI-AESTHETIC (AA) Architecture is not considered with aesthetic intent, as aesthetic qualities are irrelevant to and even harmful to architecture and society.

SUPPRESSED AESTHETICS (SU) Architecture is *secretly* considered with aesthetic intent, although resulting aesthetic qualities are described as the result of nonaesthetic considerations.

COMMUNICATORY AESTHETICS (CA) Architecture is considered with aesthetic intent such that the aesthetic qualities are intended to express a *specific* meaning that is authored by the architect, whether it be symbolic, metaphorical, narrative, nostalgic, a proof of talent, or meant to convey relevance by being for or against a current architectural "style."

FORMALIST AESTHETICS (FA) Architecture is considered with aesthetic intent such that the aesthetic qualities are intended to produce feelings of pleasure in the viewer.

SPECULATIVE AESTHETICS (SA) Architecture is considered with aesthetic intent such that the aesthetic qualities convey a gestalt sense of the set of ideals that the designer has for the future of the built environment. This requires an acceptance that architects *can never know in advance* the social and cultural impact of their work, but that does not mean that their work cannot aim toward just social and cultural goals.

The Anti-Aesthetic

ANTI-AESTHETIC (AA) Architecture is not considered with aesthetic intent, as aesthetic qualities are irrelevant to and even harmful to architecture and society.

THE ANTI-AESTHETIC is the default position with regard to aesthetics within architectural theory and practice today, as has been outlined previously. One could make the claim that the proto-anti-aesthetic position could be found in Plato's *Republic* where, as described by theorist Michael Young, Plato "feared the forsaking of moral essence through the seduction of the senses, in other words, ethics compromised by aesthetics."[1] An AA position assumes, as previously noted, that aesthetic qualities, often visual, are either superficial or used by those in power to nefariously hide otherwise visible truths. This accounting produces architectural forms that have aesthetic properties that are not determined by an architect intentionally but are rather an aftereffect of the solutions to the functional problems as present-

1. For Young's description see Michael Young, "Fear of the Mediated Image," *The Cornell Journal of Architecture,* no. 11 (August 25, 2019): 146–61.

ed by the client. That is not to say that architecture developed within the AA framework does not have aesthetic qualities, only that they should be of no concern to the architect.

The AA position within architecture has not only more than a century of momentum within the profession but has also received contemporary support in the form of adjacent theoretical positions that advocate for a similar stance, notably that of *indifference*, as introduced by architectural theorist Michael Meredith, primarily his article *Indifference, Again*.[2] In this article Meredith advocates for what he describes as techniques that are "*anti-aesthetic* . . . through an acceptance of non-design: the banal, generic, and unoriginal." In a later response to this article, I identify multiple problems with Meredith's position, which can be summed up in his own words as "employing anti-aesthetic aesthetics of appropriation, ready-mades, and lists." He is more specific about the formal architectural agenda of the project of indifference and writes regarding its associated architects that "they play, collect, scroll, re-appropriate, and reuse, taking little interest in tabula rasa innovation or authorial originality."[3]

At the root of all of my disagreements with this position is the fact that the position of *indifference* to aesthetic qualities is nearly synonymous with any historic AA position, but also that this produces an inherent contradiction that is evident in all AA positions; notably that one cannot design *anti-aesthetically* in the same way that one cannot hum *antimusically*, because the act of humming is always musical, even if it is only the humming of single note. One cannot "unhum" with one's mouth as a way to counter the musicality of humming. If one is considering aes-

2. See his original article: Michael Meredith, "Indifference, Again," *Log* 39 (Winter 2017): 75–79, as well as my response in the following issue titled "Speculation vs. Indifference," found in *Log* 40 (Spring/Summer 2017): 121–35.

3. Meredith, *Indifference, Again*, 78.

thetics, even by trying to *look* nonaesthetically considered, one is, by definition, working aesthetically, and therefore cannot be designing anti-aesthetically. More clearly, while an architect can have an anti-aesthetic *theoretical* stance, one cannot *design* anti-aesthetically. Therefore, the most forceful rejection of aesthetic ambitions is to ignore them in favor of championing what is automatically produced by the systems of capitalism within which we all exist—in other words, the generic (which is still an aesthetic). As such, while the opposite of a pro-aesthetic theoretical position can be an anti-aesthetic theoretical position, the opposite of a pro-aesthetic *design* position can only be to design with the intent to be generic.

Another analogy might be to imagine an author who holds an anti-authorship theoretical position. This author could argue this position along many lines, perhaps that authorship is authoritarian, egocentric, or as Herder originally suggested, is a fallacy because it is history or a *zeitgeist* that is responsible for creative production. However, if an author were to *write* about their anti-authorship position, they would become authors and therefore be, in fact, working against their positions as they existed prior to writing. Designing *indifferently,* as Meredith champions, yields only the "banal, generic, and unoriginal"—yet to design *toward* these ends as an architect is still an *aesthetic* position. While within architecture holding such a position that valorizes the generic may provide brief personal or academic success, it seems unlikely to offer any long-term benefits as an operating strategy for architecture's relationship with the world at large. To valorize the generic is to be indifferent to appearance of the physical world, including neglecting the qualities of identity and culture that define the time in which we collectively exist.[4]

4. An alternate ancestry of the project of indifference can also be found in affect theory, which makes a brief appearance in architec-

As we have addressed the arts as being the categorial distinction most historically valued for aesthetic attention, our argument should address the Anti-Aesthetic position as it has impacted artistic practice in order to further illuminate AA's role within larger creative and architectural culture today. One significant and early modern corollary from the arts that also sought to define an AA position was Marcel Duchamp's *Fountain* sculpture—a readymade urinal placed on its side in an exhibition for the Society of Independent Artists in New York City in 1917. While the original urinal was pulled from the exhibition, the controversy it prompted led to an important inquiry: Was it art? Could anything now go in an exhibition or museum? Could art be about manipulating concepts instead of paint? These questions, in turn, opened doors for further challenges to the boundaries of art curation, be they dead sharks (Damien Hirst), starving dogs (Guillermo Vargas), or performing artists staring deeply into visitors' eyes (Marina Abramović). However, as Clement Greenberg notes, such a trick of placing a urinal into an artistic exhibition context *only works once*. The second artist to place a urinal in a gallery does not yield the same intended effects as the first, as the impact of the work is theoretical or conceptual, not aesthetic, and therefore exhausted upon its initial introduction. Were this not the case, and artists could continue to achieve fame and praise through the continual placing of urinals in galleries and museums, in which case galleries and museums would rather quickly become restrooms of unimaginable scale. The same

tural theory in the 2008 exhibition *Matters of Sensation* at the Artists Space gallery in New York City, where the curators Marcelo Spina and Georgina Huljich describes the affect-based design work with sentiments similar to those of the position of indifference (although preceding it by a decade) in that it "seeks to answer no questions, solve no problems, and broach no oppositions." Quote taken from Huljich and Spina, *Matters of Sensation: Exhibition Catalog.*

situation exists within architecture, in that an architect who produces a generic building that is championed for its cleverness or brilliance, can only be a one-off. The second architect to produce a generic building is confronted with the loss of the novelty that accompanied the original. If this were not the case, there would be a race to produce the *most generic* architecture, which itself would, ironically, be a nearly entirely aesthetic endeavor.

With these considerations in hand, I do not accept that an AA position has anything further to offer to architecture. We should disqualify the Anti-Aesthetic from being a valid position to continue to guide a new generation of architectural thought and production, independent of whether it is an AA position that emerges from Architectural Modernism, critical theory, or contemporary *indifference*. Casting aesthetic and, by extension, visual ambitions in architecture as nefarious, superficial, or unworthy of attention forces its aesthetic qualities to be defined as the formal after-effects of capitalism, or to be actually or ironically generic—all of which offer the ultimate success to merely economic concerns over cultural ones.

Suppressed Aesthetics

SUPPRESSED AESTHETICS (SU) Architecture is *secretly* considered with willful aesthetic intent, although resulting aesthetic qualities are described as the result of non-aesthetic considerations.

A SUPPRESSED AESTHETICS (SU) position may be understood as an in-between state located between an Anti-Aesthetic position and a position where aesthetic qualities are valued. Within an SU position an architect freely designs with aesthetic ambitions, but then hides these ambitions behind other narratives that are intended to describe the appearance of the building to be the result of nonaesthetic factors. I believe there are multiple contemporary architects operating, some with great professional success, according to the SU position. To operate in such a manner requires walking the fine line of designing aesthetically but never revealing one's interest in designing aesthetically or toward particular architectural appearances. Holding, consciously or unconsciously, a SU position allows a designer to have aesthetic ambitions as long as they are never discussed publicly, and the aesthetic outcome of the building is *presented* as being the after-effect of other, more serious, functional concerns.

One of the most celebrated buildings of recent decades has been the Seattle Public Library, designed by Pritzker Prize–winning architect Rem Koolhaas and his firm, Office of Metropolitan Architecture (OMA). The physical form of the building is that of a giant faceted crystal, with angular planes and sloping reflective surfaces. Koolhaas presents this unusual faceted aesthetic form as being the *inevitable* result of careful programmatic study of the interior workings of library staff. The official OMA description of the project describes these internal workings and how they produce the strange form, as follows: "The library's various programs are intuitively arranged across five platforms and four flowing 'in between' planes, *which together dictate the building's distinctive faceted shape*."[1] According to this view the aesthetic form of the building is merely a result of intense study of the needs of the client and a keen understanding of the relationships between the various functional uses, resulting in building's forceful aesthetic appearances. By taking this position and popularizing its account, Koolhaas not only benefits from appearing as an attentive architect, carefully attuned to solving functional problems in contemporary library design but is also able to resist any criticism that the building is the result of aesthetic intent, therefore inoculating him against artistic criticism.

The project designer at OMA who worked with Koolhaas on the Seattle project was Joshua Prince Ramus. In a public debate I had with Prince-Ramus, later published as the article "You Are Playing a Fool's Game: A Public Exchange between Mark Foster Gage and Joshua Prince-Ramus on Museum Plaza and Beauty,"

1. My italics. See Rem Koolhaas, "Seattle Central Library: Project Description," as featured on the official Office for Metropolitan Architecture website: https://www.oma.com/projects/seattle-central -library.

he rather directly defined the SU position that he and Koolhaas operated within when he stated (rather surprisingly to me at the time) that "you still have your own personal aesthetic agenda, but that is not what you are debating with the client."[2] Further along in our debate, as also noted in the article, he stated, "It is much more powerful to know what you think is beautiful and be able to justify it on issues that simply have nothing to do with that."[3] There is some irony in the fact that the then–architecture critic of the *New York Times,* Herbert Muschamp, described the building, in *aesthetic* terms, as "big rock candy mountain of a building."[4] I find the accuracy of his claim unimpeachable.

Any nonarchitectural observer of this visually massive crystalline gem of a building set in the heart of downtown Seattle would be hard-pressed to extract the fact of the building's radical form from intricate functional concerns. This is because nonarchitect observers and users of buildings judge them *aesthetically.* For most users, the knowledge of a building's "creation story" will never become apparent by simply viewing the final structure. Prince-Ramus said as much when he noted, "Far and away, the largest reaction to it during design was, 'It is terribly ugly, and it is going to blight the city.' . . . the general public did not inform themselves of the ideas behind the project or understand its performative ambitions." As is visible in this statement, it is the public's responsibility to "inform themselves" of the ideas of the project, rather than be allowed to judge it aesthetically without

2. Joshua Prince-Ramus and Mark Foster Gage, "You Are Playing a Fool's Game: A Public Exchange between Mark Foster Gage and Joshua Prince-Ramus on Museum Plaza and Beauty," *Perspecta* 40, no. 7 (October 2007): 102–3.

3. Prince-Ramus and Gage.

4. Herbert Muschamp, "The Library That Puts on Fishnets and Hits the Disco," *New York Times,* May 16, 2004, Architecture section: 1–3.

the input of the architect—despite the fact that it occupies a full and very public block within downtown Seattle.

Suppressed Aesthetics inoculates architects against aesthetic criticism because by assuming such a position they are making no aesthetic claims or, as is the case with Koolhaas and Prince-Ramus, ever even referring to the formal, visual, or aesthetic properties of the building—despite the building obviously having incredibly significant formal and aesthetic properties. The architect who operates in this mode is free to explore any aesthetic directions so long as they are hidden within other narratives. The reason why SU is problematic should be obvious: it is predicated on the manipulation of the truth for personal gain, either economically or egotistically. Furthermore, SU seems to offer, at least in the case of Koolhaas, disdain for the general public of viewers who judge the building aesthetically as opposed to "informing themselves" regarding the architect-prescribed functional narrative of the building. I believe it to be self-evident that the SU position, being predicated on distain for the public and the withholding and manipulation of truth, offers no fertile ground for any architecture that has positive ethical and moral aspirations for the future of the built environment.

Communicatory Aesthetics

The single biggest problem in communication is the illusion that it has taken place.

—GEORGE BERNARD SHAW

COMMUNICATORY AESTHETICS (CA) Architecture is considered with aesthetic intent such that the aesthetic qualities are intended to express a *specific* meaning that is authored by the architect, whether it be symbolic, metaphorical, narrative, nostalgic, a proof of talent, or meant to convey relevance by being for or against a current architectural "style."

THE COMMUNICATORY AESTHETICS position is the first self-consciously and honestly *willful* aesthetic category in our developing lexicon of aesthetic modes of architectural engagement. CA is likely the aesthetic category most familiar to nonarchitects, where the building is intended to convey, through aesthetic properties, a particular meaning as intended by the architect. Through the design of form, color, material, and texture, it is then assumed that this intended meaning may be extracted by the viewing public. The aesthetic ambitions of the project are therefore focused on the act of communication.

The types of meaning intended to be conveyed are too numerous to be addressed in full, but a brief accounting will be useful in illustrating the concept.

Imagine an architect designing a building from scratch, with total control over the aesthetic appearance of the final structure. If the architect chooses to avoid both the previously addressed AA and SU positions, they are then choosing not only to author the aesthetic appearance of the building but also take credit for this authorship. This inherently engages the architect's ego, as the aesthetic qualities of the building will be judged against the stated intent of the architect. This, in turn, places the architect in the vulnerable position of needing to express something that is worth expressing, but also of expressing something valued by those who will evaluate the project, be they users, observers, or critics. It is unlikely, then, that an architect would ever choose to design the aesthetic qualities of the building to convey ethically challenging or unjust ideas deplored by users, observers, or critics. To my knowledge there have been no contemporary buildings (thankfully) celebrated for conveying abstract messages such as racism, oppression, or suffering. Similarly, there have been no buildings celebrated for looking like more culturally charged objects—no toilet buildings, Coronavirus molecule buildings, AK-47 buildings, or rotten fruit buildings. Therefore, when architects express messages through the aesthetic qualities of a building, they tend to be simple, for ease of understanding, and always positive messages. For instance, if an architect chooses to express their commitment to ecological sustainability, they make evident their use of recycled materials or sustainable technologies such as solar panels or bamboo. If an architect chooses to express their belief that the architecture and urbanism of past eras were better than those of the current era, they will design in a historical style. If an architect wishes to express their own individual talent and creativity, they will design the building to look unique when compared to other buildings of similar use by other architects. If the architect seeks to convey an even more specific meaning, the building will be designed as an easily interpreted symbol to represent that meaning.

Buildings that are intended to convey symbolic meanings through aesthetic composition are common today, as there is an ease in designing a symbol that automatically associates the building with a positive message. It is more difficult to criticize a building designed as peace sign and dedicated to world peace than it is to criticize a gun-shaped skyscraper to house Academi, formerly known as Xe, formerly known as Blackwater, which provides mercenary services to the U.S. government. An example of such saccharine symbolic appropriation can be found in the work of another Pritzker prize–winning architect, Daniel Libeskind, who when designing the jagged and angular Denver Art Museum said he was inspired by the "rocky and jagged cliffs of the Rockies." Therefore, when the viewer sees the building, they are intended to extract "rocky and jagged cliffs of the Rockies" from the aesthetic properties of the building—its appearance. In this case the aesthetic properties of the building were composed aesthetically to mimic local geological formations, and therefore having an association with local geology is what is being communicated. If this message is properly extracted, what is there to criticize about geology? Who in Denver, Colorado, could possibly find fault with the desire to be associated with grand and natural mountains? The problem, however, is that the aesthetic qualities of the building are not being judged, only its appearance when compared to a "jagged cliff of the Rockies." Therefore, an architect who designs the aesthetic properties of a building to support a symbolic reading is able to transfer any critique of the building's aesthetic appearance to whether or not it conjures its symbolic intent.

A more saccharine[1] example of a CA position comes from architectural designer and engineer Santiago Calatrava, who in his design of the US$4 billion World Trade Center Transportation Hub in lower Manhattan composed the building to look like a dove being released from the hands of a child. The reason given was that children represent innocence, and doves represent peace—and that the violence of the World Trade Center destruction that occurred on 9/11 required the healing presence of innocence and peace on the site. Therefore, the appearance of "doveness" and the symbolic relationship between doves and peace was intended to be communicated by the aesthetic properties of the building, and so the building was given giant "wings" that cantilever over the adjacent streets.

There are countless other examples of the composition of aesthetic properties being used similarly to convey symbolism within architecture, but this strategy comes with its own drawbacks. Two unavoidable problems become apparent when designing with a CA position that forces aesthetic properties to act in the service of direct communication. The first is that the messages are limited to being infantilizing and simple. One is not sure how the communication of ideas such as "rocky" or "dovey" are intended to improve urban communities or the human condition. At best, architecture is capable of conveying one-liners that seem unconvincingly simplistic in a world where other forms of communication, such as smartphones, can convey encyclopedias of information instantly. To use architecture as a communication device in a society defined by the continual emergence of more effective communication devices seems to me to be a misuse of architecture as well as the aesthetic qualities it is capable of exploring.

1. Borrowing the term from Peter Eisenman's "Duck Soup" where he similarly describes this work. Eisneman, "Duck Soup," *Log* 7 (Winter/Spring 2006): 141.

A second problem emerges with the CA position when the message is, though simple, still irretrievable by all viewers. In this case only those with the knowledge of the meaning are capable of interpreting it, meaning that only those with a certain education are invited to participate in the architecture. Once again we can return to an excerpt of the quote by the Seattle Public Library project architect Joshua Prince Ramus, who stated that "the general public did not *inform themselves* of the ideas behind the project."[2] This is a rather elite proposition, to suggest that the aesthetic qualities of an architectural project are reserved only for those with the education required to correctly interpret them or have the time to go retrieve such information. Architecture, after all, rarely comes with an instruction booklet that outlines the communicatory message meant to be received, so that unless a viewer comes prepared with the information required to decipher the meaning, the meaning will sometimes simply not be received. An observer who does not know that bamboo panels are recycled will not glean the architect's sustainable intent. A tourist visiting downtown Manhattan will likely not see the new transit station and make the connection that it looks like a dove being released from the hands of a child, or that the (unrecognized) dove represents peace and the (unrecognized) child's hands represent innocence—and that these associations are supposed to be healing devices when they are located on a site destroyed by a terrorist attack decades prior. In fact, the reverse seems to be true, with the transit station most commonly being compared to the skeleton of a dead whale.

A Communicatory Aesthetics position used as a strategy to guide aesthetic production seems to hold little promise for the future of architecture, as architecture is simply not a very good

2. Gage and Prince-Ramus, "You Are Playing a Fool's Game," 102–3.

communication device when compared with the contemporary alternatives. More than one billion smartphones are sold each year, each with the capacity to communicate information in vast quantities and near-instant speeds. To request that architecture continue to operate as a communication tool in the same manner it did four millennia ago is an absurd proposition. It also limits architecture to having its aesthetic properties appropriated by simplistic one-liners, thereby inhibiting the freedom of architects to be more aesthetically speculative. With the compounding benefits of the printing press, increased literacy, the telephone, the computer, the internet, the aforementioned smartphones, and social media, humanity is in possession of far more effective means of communication than architecture. To force architecture into this role in the twenty-first century is effectively to turn architecture into an anachronism, limited to conveying simplistic, even infantilizing, messages to an audience that may not be in a position even to receive them. As such, the CA position seems to hold little promise for the aesthetic aspects the newly unfolding architecture of the twenty-first century.

Formalist Aesthetics

My God, a moment of bliss. Why, isn't that enough for a whole lifetime?

—FYODOR DOSTOEVSKY, "White Nights"

FORMALIST AESTHETICS (FA) Architecture is considered with aesthetic intent such that the aesthetic qualities are intended to produce feelings of pleasure in the viewer.

IN HIS AFOREMENTIONED "Default Theory of Aesthetic Value," James Shelly defines perceptual formalism as the case where an entity is seen to have value "strictly in virtue of its perceptual properties," which he describes as primarily visual, although sometimes auditory.[1] This is a contemporary reading of a two-millennia-old definition of formalism that has roots at least as far back as Aristotle's *Eudemian Ethics,* where he outlines that sense-derived pleasures could be shared by everyone, independent of any thoughts one may have in association with the object being viewed.[2] It should be noted that, while formalism is

1. Shelley, "The Default Theory of Aesthetic Value," 1.
2. Aristotle, "Eudemian Ethics," 1214a1–1249b25.

well-trodden intellectual territory in the arts and literature, its trajectory within architectural history is somewhat different and requires some explanation in order to assess Formalist Aesthetics as a contemporary aesthetic position for architecture.

The modern concept of formalism in architecture was synthesized from Aristotle's position by the Renaissance architectural theorist Leon Battista Alberti in his 1452 book *De Re Aedificatoria,* more commonly translated as *On the Art of Building: In Ten Books.*[3] Alberti's aesthetic position is decidedly formalist, relying heavily on the use of proper proportions through what he terms *lineaments,* which function as an abstract system of organizing lines that govern a building's shape, entirely unrelated to the communication of abstract concepts.[4] In his *Ten Books* Alberti also offers the further distinction that aesthetic experience is produced by what is essential, not extraneous to the overall composition. He writes, again altering Aristotle's primarily biological ideas about "shape" for use in architecture, that "beauty is a definite proportional relationship between all parts of that to which these parts belong, so that nothing can be added, reduced, or changed, without making it less deserving of approval."[5] Alberti's writings had tremendous influence from their publication through the early twentieth century, when new efforts were made, unsuccessfully for architecture, to champion the position of aesthetic formalism against the then emerging Anti-Aesthetic positions of Architectural Modernism, later combined with the AA positions of critical theory.

3. Mitrović, "Aesthetic Formalism in Renaissance Architectural Theory," 321.

4. See Book VI of Alberti, *On the Art of Building,* 447–49. Also see Branko Mitrović, *Serene Greed of the Eye: Leon Battista Alberti and the Philosophical Foundations of Renaissance Architectural Theory* (Berlin: Deutscher Kunstverlag, 2006).

5. Alberti, 150.

In these early twentieth-century efforts to support FA we can include, in particular, Bloomsbury Group art critic Clive Bell, in particular through his essay "The Aesthetic Hypothesis," the first section in his 1914 book *Art*. In this work Bell proposes an extreme position of FA that describes a means for the reception of visual art.[6] An important aspect of this is his inclusion of architecture and objects of design as deserving of aesthetic consideration—he specifically notes a wide range of items including "pictures, pots, temples, and statues."[7] The key concept in Bell's argument is that the presence of *significant form* in a work of art, or architecture, is solely responsible for any aesthetic sensation the viewer may encounter. Bell's *significant form* relies "exclusively on the visual properties of forms and the relations of forms, including their color."[8] It is important to note that, for Bell, significant form exists independent of the viewer and is therefore a wholly objective quality.

Bell's work is included in annals of FA in architecture because he offers an important call for legible three-dimensionality in painting and architecture as, for him, the appearance of this depth more frequently leads to the aforementioned state of "aesthetic contemplation" brought about by the presence of significant form. Bell divorces the need for additional conceptual information from the process of aesthetic judgment and notes that "to appreciate a work of art we need bring with us nothing from life, no knowledge of its ideas and affairs, no familiarity

6. As a trivial aside, Clive Bell was also the brother-in-law to Virginia Woolf.

7. Bell, "The Aesthetic Hypothesis," 42.

8. Clive Bell's work on significant form has recently received new attention in the neurosciences through studies of cortical activation correlating with the experience of beauty. For this fascinating research, see Zeki, "Clive Bell's 'Significant Form' and the Neurobiology of Aesthetics."

with its emotions."[9] He further qualifies this by writing, "for the purposes of aesthetics, we have no right, neither is there any necessity, to pry behind the object into the state of mind of him who made it." Aesthetic judgment or, in his terms, aesthetic contemplation is an act utterly independent of abstracted information generated by context or proposed by the original creator, thus offering an extreme FA position—one with architectural significance in that it *explicitly* includes architectural forms as warranting FA judgments.

Perhaps the most forceful advocate of FA in architecture prior to the development of the AA positions of Architectural Modernism and the introduction of critical theory into architecture was Geoffrey Scott, an architectural historian and author of *The Architecture of Humanism: A Study in the History of Taste*.[10] Published in the same year as Bell's aforementioned book, Scott's 1914 chapter "The Mechanical Fallacy" is targeted against the scientific and mechanical narrative of the early twentieth century that sought to isolate areas of human inquiry into increasingly specialized disciplines. A significant aspect of Scott's text is that it is written *against* architecture being justified only by means of its legible structure and construction—that is to say, Architectural Modernism. For Scott, human intervention in the aesthetic qualities of architectural form is crucial and required, as our senses have their own requirements for aesthetic satisfaction that cannot be satiated with a mere conceptual understanding of structural truth. While not against "good construction" he opposes its misuse as the only criteria for aesthetic judgment, writing that the science of construction

9. Bell, 48.

10. As a trivial aside, Geoffrey Scott was one of Edith Wharton's closest friends.

is a "perhaps a natural ally, but certainly a blind master."[11] This drive toward disciplinary autonomy, which took the form of mechanical-cum-tectonic purity in the case of architecture, is the subject of Geoffrey Scott's derision as well as the body of ideas from which Architectural Modernism eventually emerges. Scott argues against the assumption that either good construction or legible structure, as is revealed in a "mechanical" aesthetic, produces beautiful or good architecture. For Scott, architecture, particularly in the era of mechanical production, must resist the temptation to be simplistically reduced to the presence of mere structure or precise means of truthful assembly. The act of judging a building aesthetically must encompass greater formal issues than what he derisively refers to as "intellectually tracing forces" (i.e., structure).[12]

After more than a century of dormancy within architecture, a valid FA position is beginning to reemerge within architectural theory. This contemporary FA position, however, should not be confused with pure *aesthetic hedonism,* which as Shelley notes is where "the aesthetic value of an object is the value it has in virtue of some pleasure it gives."[13] Aesthetic hedonism therefore is not limited to *perceptual* properties in the pursuit of offering aesthetic pleasure, as the contemporary FA position would be— as it descends from Alberti, Bell, and Scott. For instance, within a position of aesthetic hedonism, aesthetic value could come from an architect receiving pleasure from personally carving geometric shapes into the side of a building, even if the resulting forms were universally considered to be astoundingly ugly. Within aesthetic hedonism, the physical act of carving need be the only producer of pleasure that justifies the aesthetic value

11. Scott, *The Architecture of Humanism,* 120.
12. Scott, 117.
13. Shelley, "The Default Theory of Aesthetic Value," 1.

of the work. The contemporary FA position is more focused and requires pleasure to emerge from the *visual appreciation* of work purely for its perceptual aesthetic properties rather than any other form of individual pleasure it might provide, for instance within the process of its making. Therefore, FA is not aesthetic hedonism but instead considers a building's value to be contingent primarily on the pleasure it provides to those who view it, namely, its users and the community in which it exists.

Within the past two decades FA has begun to be addressed in greater detail within analytic philosophy and has attracted some cursory interest in architectural theory circles. This interest has arisen primarily through Kendall Walton's critique of what was eventually defined as *extreme aesthetic formalism* and Nick Zangwill's resulting position of *moderate aesthetic formalism.* Walton's and Zangwill's refinements to FA are made through the refining of the definition of *extreme aesthetic formalism,* which is a claim that *all* aesthetic properties of an artwork are formal, whereas within *moderate aesthetic formalism* only *some* aesthetic properties in an artwork are formal, while others are not.[14] This division somewhat echoes Immanuel Kant's distinction between free and dependent beauty found in section 16 of the *Critique of Aesthetic Judgment,* where he notes that not all appreciation of beauty is contingent on pure aesthetic judgment. Zangwill claims as much when he notes that "Kant was also a moderate formalist, who opposed extreme formalism."[15] In Kant's position, there are two facets to beauty: free beauty, which presupposes no concept, and dependent beauty, which does presuppose a concept that aesthetic judgment is rendered against. Kant's concept

14. Zangwill, "In Defence of Moderate Aesthetic Formalism."
15. Zangwill, "In Defence of Moderate Aesthetic Formalism," 82. Here Zangwill is referring to how Kant distinguishes free and dependent beauty insection16 of *The Critique of Judgement.*

of free beauty, then, is largely a precursor to the contemporary architectural aesthetic position of FA. Zangwill's further exploration of Kant holds that it is through dependent beauty that we understand the nonformal aesthetic properties of art and that "some works have non-formal aesthetic properties because of (or in virtue of) the way they *embody* some historically given non-aesthetic function."[16] For instance, picture a red circle painted on a white background. Such a painting of a red circle has aesthetic properties of *redness* and *circleness,* which are independent of more complex abstract concepts. However a nonformal aesthetic property might be that the painting is of a Japanese flag, which, as a dependent concept, determines the shape and color of the red circle against the white background for accuracy—but this flag history is not *perceivable* and is therefore a nonformal aesthetic property.

Formalist Aesthetics as a valid aesthetic position was largely exiled from the architectural theory and practice by the sequential appearance of World War I and Architectural Modernism, but it also bears the weight of more than a century of sustained critique against it. As such, it seems unlikely that such a position could be successfully resurrected into architecture in a productive manner for two reasons:

1. There is already a century of arguments and theoretical momentum within theory levied against it.
2. It, being contingent on pleasure, offers a seemingly helpless position for a contemporary architectural culture confronted

16. Zangwill, 185. For more of Zangwill's exploration of Kant and moderate aesthetic formalism, see his book, *The Metaphysics of Beauty,* which is a general defense of formalist positions that includes reprinted versions of his previous contributions to this discussion. Also see his paper "In Defence of Extreme Formalism about Inorganic Nature: Reply to Parsons," *British Journal of Aesthetics* 45:185–91.

with the global crises of inequality, climate change, and the fallout of the Coronavirus pandemic. In short, it seems tone deaf for architecture's contemporary response to a world on fire to offer only brief moments of pleasure.

That is not to suggest that an FA position is without cultural value, which I believe is not the case, but only to note that resurrecting it in a largely unaltered historic state would ultimately be a losing proposition for the future of aesthetic engagement within architecture.

Speculative Aesthetics

SPECULATIVE AESTHETICS (SA) Architecture is considered with aesthetic intent such that the aesthetic qualities convey a gestalt sense of the set of ideals that the designer has for the future of the built environment. This requires an acceptance that architects *can never know in advance* the social and cultural impact of their work, but that does not mean that their work cannot aim toward just social and cultural goals.

WITHIN A SPECULATIVE AESTHETICS position aesthetic qualities are valued, so that it is by default not an Anti-Aesthetic position. SA is also neither a Communicatory Aesthetic position, as there is no *specific* meaning to be conveyed, whether it be symbolic, metaphorical, narrative, talent-based, nostalgic, or to convey relevance by being for or against a current architectural "style," nor a purely Formalist position, in either the extreme or moderate sense of the term—as it has no corresponding ambitions toward *only* the production of pleasure via perception. Instead SA seeks to, through aesthetic qualities, primarily visual appearances, to allude through a gestalt reading to the ideals that the designer has for the future of the built environment—

as they are determined to be of value by the designer based on their experience. This cannot be a definitive claim but rather an acknowledgment as an ambition that may fail. In my previously noted conversation with Jacques Rancière he described this aspect of aesthetic practice as follows:

> The artistic is about the implementation of an idea. It implies some kind of anticipation of the result, which may be put to the extreme in the case of political art. *Instead, the aesthetic means that you don't exactly know what will be the effect of what you are doing.*

An SA position within architecture offers multiple advantages for architectural theory and practice when compared to the previously described positions of Anti-Aesthetic (AA), Suppressed Aesthetics (SU), Communicatory Aesthetics (CA), and Formalist Aesthetics (FA). These are briefly outlined as follows:

1. SA, unlike AA, allows for the consideration of aesthetic properties in establishing the cultural value of architecture.
2. SA, unlike SU, allows for aesthetic discourse and discussion to occur *in the open*, unsecreted, and has no inherent position of disdain for the public of viewers and users.
3. SA, unlike CA, allows for the production and conveyance of virtue and meaning without resorting to simplistic messages, single-authored intent, or the requirement for an educated and correct interpretation.
4. SA, unlike FA, allows for the possibility of nonhedonistic formal pleasure, without such formal pleasure being the *primary* qualification for architectural value.

Based solely upon the cursory consideration outlined above, we can conclude that SA offers value for consideration among its peer categories, and it may surpass them in contemporary relevance as it is the only option not limited to the pursuit of pure pleasure and allows for aesthetic intention containing both virtue and ideals without reducing such intentions to simplistic communication devices.

In this, SA shares some features with the larger contemporary movement toward *virtue aesthetics,* which as described by Alan T. Wilson "encourages a re-focusing of philosophical attention onto the aesthetic character traits and qualities of agents, in the same way that virtue ethics and virtue epistemology have encouraged us to focus on *moral* and *intellectual* character traits."[1] SA, however, is not entirely synonymous with *virtue aesthetics,* because such positions, as Tom Roberts suggests, contain and require *aesthetic faculty virtues,* which refer primarily to aesthetic talents of the individual, such as "skill with drawing" or "perfect pitch," that are less germane to the subject of architecture, as it is a collaborative enterprise.[2] Instead, SA primarily adopts from *virtue aesthetics* Roberts' concept of *aesthetic trait virtues* which are all *character* traits that are not contingent on the agent's faculties, but rather their intent, and can include virtues of the creative individual such as "aesthetic forms of generosity, honesty and authenticity."[3]

This SA position I am articulating also integrates a key component of Jacques Ranciere's ideas about equality: that creative practices cannot start out with the ambition to repair inequalities but rather must assume that equality exists as a condition of their origins. To return to my conversation with Rancière, he notes the unsure quality of designing equality as a fix versus taking it as a starting point. SA can assume equality as a starting

1. While important work on virtue philosophy and virtue aesthetics has been done by figures such as Rosalind Hursthouse, Roger Pouivet, Michael Slote, and Chrisine Swanton, I take this more recent aesthetic definition from Alan Wilson in his 2020 article, "The Virtue of Aesthetic Courage," 455.

2. Roberts, "Aesthetic Virtues: Traits and Faculties."

3. Roberts, 443.

point without endeavoring to fix all of society's ills. Rancière recounted to me that

> At this point we meet the problem of the egalitarian purposes of architecture. I think that it evinces a kind of double bind. On the one hand, there was this architectural dream to promote equality though design and through building. *But equality cannot be a product; it must be a point of departure.* That is the first point.[4]

The emphasis on designers' speculative ambitions toward a more just built environment, rather than the production of *specific* but necessarily simplistic virtuous messages that are intended to emerge from form is a defining characteristic of SA. In SA, therefore, the virtue and ideals are located in the designer's intent rather than being "correctly" extractable from architectural form. That does not mean that such architectural form does not have virtuous effects, only that it is not the responsibility of architectural form to convey such virtuous intent through direct messaging. In short, architecture may, through an

---

4. He continued: "The second point is that in architecture, this idea of promoting equality through design was based itself on a certain sociology. Architecture was part of this big project with the genius architects of the Werkbund and the Bauhaus, etc. But this big activist project of reshaping all forms of life was more-or-less based on the idea that equality was brought by the social and economic process itself. This idea was very powerful in the sociological tradition: the idea that modernity means a homogenization of the conditions of life, which means equality. . . . The architectural dream—I think—was based on this idea that equality comes by itself, by the very process of modern life. It was the presupposition even under the Marxist theory that equality is marching with the transformations of production. We know now that that was not at all the case. Buildings that were supposed to promote equality were based on this idea of modernization. And now those cities are just ghettos for drugs, criminality, and now terrorism. This is not a critique of architecture, but the point is that it is not a question of functionalism versus nonfunctionalism. It is this double relation or double play with equality."

SA position, freely deploy aesthetic intent with the ambition that architecture *act* toward a more just present and future, without claiming success in advance, rather than merely *appearing* to do so in the present.

If an architect is operating within an SA framework contingent on agent virtue, they are less likely to be either intentionally or unintentionally doing harm to the built environment. An SA position therefore has the dual function of providing a platform for aesthetic speculation and can also act as a failsafe against doing harm through architectural design or its negligence. Furthermore, the inclusion of virtue within an aesthetic position allows one working within an SA framework to have formal and aesthetic interests that operate above the level of pleasure but below the level of enforcing immediate communication-based resolution, as CA requires. As such, SA can be both formalist and communicatory, whereby formalism can still operate in the pursuit of pleasure via perception, and the communicatory aspect of architecture is lodged in architects' larger moral intent rather than acting merely as a messaging device for one-liners, such as "rockiness" or "doveness."

An SA position requires of designers what Wilson refers to as *aesthetic courage,* which seems a precisely calibrated response to its opposite within architecture—a Suppressed Aesthetic (SU) position—where aesthetic intent is hidden so that the architect can avoid criticism in aesthetic registers. SU therefore is a position of vulnerability, and as an anti-SU position, SA requires the possibility of personal risk, called "courage," which within architecture today would be to open oneself to aesthetic critique of one's work. Wilson suggests, however, that this vulnerability to critique is, in fact, one of the operating characteristics of *aesthetic courage* and would also be active within an SA position within architecture. He writes that an artist, or by extension an architect, who is willing to endure hardships in order to create an aesthetically valuable series of works has a better chance of succeeding than one who is easily defeated when faced with the prospect of personal risk.[5]

The benefit of assuming such risk is that designing with an SA goal, in not describing an absolute future outcome, allows for a more participatory role of the viewer—which we will call *curiosity*. Curiosity can be generated by aesthetic operations by allowing for a limited formalism of intent unencumbered by the need to provide specific meanings or solutions to current problems. Put another way, curiosity is an invitation to future users and viewers of a work of architecture to participate in its interpretation and meaning instead of being provided with it. This has the added effect of increasing the amount of attention given to the structures of our built environment. When in a curious state, a person becomes attentive, receptive, investigatory, and alert to information, and so an SA position prompts in viewers the desire to become more attentive, receptive, investigatory, and alert to the built environment that defines the visual backdrop of their contemporary urban reality.

Architects need to think in these more expansive terms enabled in Speculative Aesthetics in order to prompt higher-fidelity observation and questioning about the very nature of our reality itself and what we, as individuals, communities, countries, and as a species, want it to be moving forward. This requires of architecture the need to be a curiosity-generating device within contemporary culture—a key aspect of an SA position, for it may only be through curiosity that architecture can keep alive its cultural value and more justly participate in the creation of new and nourishing human environments.

5. Wilson, "The Virtue of Aesthetic Courage," 463.

Conclusion, or The Appearance of the Unknown

The great cultural project . . . may very well be to rescue what we have of the art and aesthetic of religion while discarding the supernatural.

—CHRISTOPHER HITCHENS, *The Four Horsemen*

IF ONE THING has been revealed in the past decade it is that the former foundations for architecture's ethical speculation, contingent as they were on the modernist conveyance of "truth" of construction and "transparency" of program, have largely disintegrated, requiring a vast overhaul of the discipline's intellectual and ethical assumptions. Architecture can no longer continue to base its moral stance on outdated concepts of Architectural Modernism that were developed almost exclusively in a world before computers and smartphones, not to mention the input of more diverse voices. Accordingly, architects can no longer rely on the related Modernist truths that are no longer recognized, hierarchies that no longer exist, or democracies that are no longer equal. Beyond the dictates of Modernism lies something different—perhaps a still developing post–Aesthetic Turn reality for all involved in the world of design and therefore the design of the world. To imagine this requires a curiosity that pierces our common superficial understanding of reality—a curiosity uniquely specific to a speculatively aesthetic position.

I would suggest that, instead of asking of architecture to "raise awareness" of aspects of contemporary reality already thoroughly better covered in other mediums, or expecting architecture to somehow be an arbiter of the truth of reality, that the discipline recapture its earlier relationship with *the unknowable*—the one category of human experience that can be relied on to produce curiosity, and to which all humans have exactly equal access, which is to say, none. This is an inverse of a similar sentiment noted by Spinoza when he writes, "In so far as the mind sees things in their eternal aspect, it participates in eternity."[1]

The role of designed objects to act as mediators between the human and the unknowable has, in fact, been a foundational aspect of architecture, largely used in the service of religion, and has only been eclipsed since the Enlightenment through the axiomatic belief that all knowledge is, through the mechanizations of humans and science, eventually obtainable. Attentively designed objects within this framework have, as they can all be understood through science, significantly lost the ability to be intellectually or emotionally transporting, invoke curiosity, or prompt contemplation, which would all be the goals of an SA position. Instead, objects in contemporary society are more mundanely positioned as being *pre-understood*, primarily as material products that confer status or fulfill a particular human need through a particular function—as is blindingly apparent in the non-SA aesthetic positions within architecture. Yet designed objects, a category in which we can include buildings at one extreme of scale, have a well-documented history of production

1. Durant, 367.

toward other, more intangible goals, where they are not seen merely as "things" but rather as openings into alternative modes of speculative perception—as is the stated goal of SA. While such ambitions have historically been used in the service of religion and the visual arts, they may also be reconsidered toward contemporary architectural ends. Regarding the ability for objects throughout history to prompt such responses, *New York Review of Books* journalist Peter Brown, describing historic reliquaries and religious artifacts, writes:

> They are no longer considered mere decoration. We have realized that somehow, in a mute manner that partly escapes the conscious mind (and that largely escaped rationalization by theologians), the very texture of the materials used and their ingenious fashioning helped to bridge the chasm between the seen and unseen. . . . We must cease to see a mere shimmer of gold and jewels. Instead, we are looking at objects from where one world meets and elevates the other.[2]

In the first century BCE, Greek essayist (later with Roman citizenship) Plutarch observed in *De Auditu* that "the mind is not a vessel to be filled, but a fire to be kindled." This sentiment opposes the Enlightenment position where man is charged with the discovery of true knowledge and, accordingly, the "filling" of the vessel of the mind. Plutarch's "kindling" of the mind rather than its "filling" describes the human capacity for curiosity and speculation, which can be invoked and inflamed through architectural design.

Such ambitions toward the production of curiosity are not inherently religious in nature, and as such this sentiment should not be confused as being in any way in support of a reintroduction of religion into architecture. Instead, the act of prompting

2. Peter Brown, "The Glow of Byzantium," *The New York Review,* July 14, 2016: 37.

curiosity via a speculatively aesthetic position can be a power of incalculable value to the establishment of an absolute baseline of social equality—as it is both a shared and inexhaustible resource to which all of humanity has equal access. Rancière reminds us of the importance of beginning our actions with such an equitable baseline. While this does not mean that such choreographies can ever constitute anywhere near the full efforts of architectural design, they might provide an influential conceptual starting point for design that is not reliant on reductively understood data as found in a CA position—but rather a moment were designer and future users are, for the moment of design instigation, equal in their incomplete ability to fully understand the object, building, or world that they are about to share, always limited, access.

The existing nonaesthetic architectural discourses of the critical and the pseudo-scientific within architecture aim to produce a closure of knowledge and in doing so refuse such equalizing invitations to curiosity. Einstein reminds us that "it is a miracle that curiosity survives formal education," and perhaps it is even more of a miracle today if it can survive architectural education in particular, so procedural and reductive it has become. Knowledge is, of course, required for architecture to function, remain stable, properly use resources, and provide shelter; yet the sum of these requirements and of its many other responsibilities can also collectively aim toward the goals of producing a more ethically beautiful and just reality via architecture. As with the aforementioned objects, architecture can become more than a merely known and understood physical construction or object, and instead an opening into an alternative way of seeing the world—a speculation, inherently aesthetic in nature.

Architecture has the unique ability—even responsibility—to, as David Ruy suggests, be the "first thing that tells what reality looks like."[3] Architecture can produce speculatively aesthetic qualities that are not knowledge per se, but rather allusions to more distant unknown aspects of the real—the pursuit of which inspires the fires of Plutarch and becomes an ethical reminder of our shared perceptual position within humanity and the limits of its perceptual reach. Architecture that is "about" individual criteria—whether articulated critically, scientifically, or even within an aesthetic position such as CA—prohibits such explorations into higher orders of collective and shared inquiry and produces final closure once the "information" the building is intended to communicate is so received by the (only properly educated) observer. This is an act of finality, of submission, where further inquiry is repressed in the name of completed understanding. This heretical pact by which the architect determines official meaning, and the observer properly receives it, limits the ability for architecture as a discipline to allude to the vagaries of reality and to suggest new possibilities the physical constructs of a speculative future.

If not all criteria can be addressed in a design solution, then to choose any one or a selected few is to ignore all of other the possible points of intellectual or emotional entry that architecture might elicit. The extensive breadth of architecture's potential reach is one of its greatest creative and ethical assets, and to subject it to such reductiveness is a repression of the imagination and diminishes its potential to be understood within countless other speculative scenarios. As has been previously described, acts of such selective analyses are more often than not artistic decisions masquerading as scientific ones; yet they force the building to be read along the lines of the latter rather than the former. Judging or explaining a building against reductively scientific criteria is automatically dismissive of any aesthetic

3. Ruy, "Returning to (Strange) Objects."

speculation it might prompt in the viewer, as the aesthetic is, as we have seen in the common AA position, assumed to be antithetical to the truths of the scientific.

Such nonaesthetic and reductively scientific and functional goals for design are rarely purely scientific, for to be so they would require postconstruction analysis of their efficacy in order to conform to the stringent requirements of the scientific method. Instead, most fall into the ineffective and exhausted pattern of diagnosis and repair, where a selected problem is observed, and it becomes the defining ambition of the architect to solve it through design, at the expense of addressing a host of other possible problems. Accordingly, such solutions are required to be simplified into a graphic for easy digestion by the client and public (SU or CA). They also, when presented through such requisite diagrams, train the public to view architecture in decidedly nonaesthetic, primarily AA, terms—terms that produce near-immediate closure. Architecture here is seen as a simple solution to simply identified problems rather than an opportunity for collective curiosity and other forms of speculative and aesthetic conjecture.

Through accepting the inequitable basis and hierarchical procedures of the critical, or the reductively and often falsely scientific, architecture is limited to being solution based rather than aesthetically engaged as an open-ended instigator of allusive curiosity in which all can indefinitely participate—the ultimate direction of an SA position. The demystification of architecture, through its shift into a discipline of transferrable intellectual content rather than one perceived through speculatively aesthetic experience, has been observed in a larger cultural context by Steven Shaviro, who notes that

> Science is now in the process of scrubbing psychology from the human world, just as it previously scrubbed psychology from

the natural world. That is to say, the psyche itself is rapidly being de-psychologized, as paradoxical as this might sound, even
the decentering's of subjectivity proposed by psychoanalysis and
deconstruction have not really prepared us for this eventuality.[4]

He continues to describe how this leads to the undermining of

common intuitions about our own inner sensations, or what the
philosophers call qualia. . . . that there is a certain vividness and
intensity to my inner life. But this qualitative dimension of my experience is something that I cannot capture and put into words.[5]

It is the aesthetically qualitative that architecture has neglect-
ed in the service of the nonaesthetic via the scientifically and
critically quantifiable, both of which are today considered to be
equally creatively and functionally legitimizing. It is not being
argued that architecture return to only the phenomenology of
individual qualitative experience, nor to any form of religious
piety, but rather that through a new aesthetically derived equitable SA baseline, prompted through curiosity rather than
reductive statements of symbolism (CA) or hidden aesthetic
agendas (SU), architecture can shed the conventions that rely
on meaning derived from privileged insight to be established by
architects upon proverbial pedestals—and observers who are
required to be appropriately educated to decipher such meanings. Instead, as a new baseline for action, architecture can be
liberated to emphasize collective experiences of curiosity toward
the unknown and inaccessible.

While rote understanding of defined criteria will always play
a role within the discipline of architecture, it need not define
every aspect of it. There is value in aesthetic speculation and

4. Shaviro, *Discognition,* 106.
5. Shaviro, 106.

the curiosity it can produce, as there is value in the equitably empowering ability for all to access such speculation equally, without the requirement of a "correct" understanding. Being unsure, despite Enlightenment claims toward the contrary, can itself be a path to new forms of speculation about the status of reality for humanity, and it may even be the trait that best defines us. An architecture that seeks to begin its processes through this equalizing position of curiosity about the unknown might not only prompt reconsiderations of our commonly shared traits but lead toward new understandings of the nature of our physical and social environments.[6]

Aesthetics, and specifically Speculative Aesthetics (SA) within architecture are not determined to be successful or not successful based *only* on immediate pleasure given, although it may still provide immediate pleasure. An SA position is also not judged successful or not based *only* on the immediate consumption of a simplistic message, although it may communicate. Rather an SA position allows the aesthetic impact of architecture to unfold into its communities more slowly, over time, relying on the best intentions, virtues, and especially the aesthetic courage of the designer toward their realization. SA allows for an interest in aesthetics, form, and the desire to produce pleasure but is also infused with the desire to use aesthetic intent to produce curiosity and therefore invite speculation toward the production of a more virtuous and perceptually humane built reality. This also allows architecture to become *more* speculative, in that it is relieved of the obligation that the final form perform only in the present to produce pleasure or clearly broadcast a simple positive or virtuous message.

6. Some text in this section was published in an earlier iteration in Mark Foster Gage, "East of Reality: On the Granular Perception of Architecture," *PLAT Journal* 9 (2020): 1–14.

The purpose of this text is not to write the final definition of Speculative Aesthetics but rather to offer it as a possibility for consideration as a platform for additional contributions over time, all part of a larger multidisciplinary emerging effort to reintroduce aesthetics into architecture, but without inheriting the liabilities of previous aesthetic positions. It is my hope that a Speculative Aesthetic position can be fruitful territory for future developments—and offer a springboard to reconsider the value of aesthetics in the future production of our built environment. Among its peers, the Speculative Aesthetic position seems to offer the most promise, in that it liberates designers, through not only function but also aesthetics, to speculate on a more complete image of the future of our physical reality and therefore the appearance of the world.

Acknowledgments

Special thanks to all those philosophers who tolerate discussions with architects. In my case this especially includes Graham Harman, Jacques Rancière, Timothy Morton, Branko Mitrovic, and David Chalmers.

Selected Bibliography

Alberti, Leon Battista. *On the Art of Building: In Ten Books,* trans. Joseph Rykwert, Neil Leach, and Robert Tavernor. Cambridge, Mass.: MIT Press, 1991.

Aristotle. "Eudemian Ethics." In *The Complete Works of Aristotle,* ed. Jonathan Barnes, 1922–82. Princeton, N.J.: Princeton University Press, 1995.

Bell, Clive. "The Aesthetic Hypothesis." In *Art,* 3–37. 1914; repr., London, Jefferson Publication, 2015.

Carson, Allen. *Aesthetics and the Environment: Art and Architecture. New York: Routledge,* 2000.

Corbusier, Le. *Towards a New Architecture.* San Diego: Brewer, Warren & Putnam, 2014.

Dickie, George. "The New Institutional Theory of Art." In *Proceedings of the 8th Wittgenstein Symposium* 10 (1983), 57–64.

Durant, Will. *The Story of Philosophy: The Lives and Opinions of the Great Philosophers of the Western World.* New York: Simon & Schuster, 1961.

Fuksas, Massimiliano. *Less Aesthetics More Ethics: The 7th International Venice Architectural Architecture.* New York: Rizzoli, 2000.

Gage, Mark Foster. *Aesthetics Equals Politics: New Discourses across Art, Architecture, and Philosophy.* Cambridge, Mass.: MIT Press, 2019.

Gage, Mark Foster. *Aesthetic Theory: Essential Texts.* New York: Norton, 2011.

Gage, Mark Foster. *Designing Social Equality: Architecture, Aesthetics, and the Perception of Democracy.* New York: Routledge, 2019.

Gage, Mark Foster, and Joshua Prince Ramus. "You Are Playing a Fools Game: A Public Exchange between Mark Foster Gage and

Joshua Prince-Ramus on Museum Plaza and Beauty." *Perspecta* 40 (October 7, 2007): 102–3.

Gage, Mark Foster. "East of Reality: On the Granular Perception of Architecture." *PLAT Journal,* no. 9 (2020).

Gage, Mark Foster. "Speculation vs. Indifference." *Log: Contemporary Observations on the City,* no. 40 (2017).

Gaskell, Ivan. "Works of Art and Mere Real Things—Again." *British Journal of Aesthetics* 60, no. 2 (April 20, 2020): 131–49.

Hanslick, Eduard. *Eduard Hanslick's "On the Musically Beautiful": A New Translation.* Trans. Lee A. Rothfarb. Oxford: Oxford University Press, 2018.

Hays, K. Michael. Introduction to *Architecture Theory since 1968.* Cambridge, Mass.: MIT Press, 1998.

Hill, Richard. *Designs and Their Consequences: Architecture and Aesthetics.* New Haven, Conn.: Yale University Press, 1999.

Hopkins, Robert, and Nick Riggle. "Artistic Style as the Expression of Ideals." *Philosophers' Imprint* 21, no. 8 (May 2021): 1–18.

Huljich, Georgina, and Marcelo Spina. *Matters of Sensation: Exhibition Catalog.* New York: Artists Space, 2008.

Kant, Immanuel. *The Critique of Judgement.* Trans. James Creed Meredith. Oxford: A & D Publishing, 2018.

Koolhaas, Rem. "Seattle Central Library: Project Description." *Office for Metropolitan Architecture,* https://www.oma.com/projects/seattle-central-library.

Lamarque, Peter, and Stein Haugom Olsen. "Introduction." In *Aesthetics and the Philosophy of Art the Analytic Tradition: An Anthology.* Hoboken, N.J.: Wiley Blackwell, 2019.

Levinson, Jerrold. *The Pleasures of Aesthetics: Philosophical Essays.* Ithaca, N.Y.: Cornell University Press, 1996.

Macey, David. *The Penguin Dictionary of Critical Theory* London: Penguin, 2001.

Mitrović, Branko. "Aesthetic Formalism in Renaissance Architectural Theory." *Zeitschrift Für Kunstgeschichte* 66, no. 3 (2003): 321.

Muschamp, Herbert. "The Library That Puts on Fishnets and Hits the Disco." *New York Times,* May 16, 2004: 1–3.

Pedersen, Martin, and Steven Bingler. "How to Rebuild Architecture." *New York Times,* December 14, 2014: https://www.nytimes.com/2014/12/16/opinion/how-to-rebuild-architecture.html.

Penrose, Francis C. *Investigation of the Principles of Athenian Architecture: The Results of a Survey Conducted Chiefly with Reference to the Optical Refinements Exhibited in the Construction of the Ancient Buildings at Athens,* 2nd ed. Washington D.C.: McGrath, 1973.

Selected Bibliography

Plato. *The Republic*. Trans. C. J. Emlyn-Jones and William Preddy. Cambridge, Mass.: Harvard University Press, 2013.

Roberts, Tom. "Aesthetic Virtues: Traits and Faculties." *Philosophical Studies* 175, no. 2 (2017): 429–47.

Ruy, David. "Returning to (Strange) Objects." Southern California Institute for Architecture: 2013 Public Lecture Series. January 30, 2013. W. M. Keck Lecture Hall. Los Angeles, California.

Saito, Yuriko. *Aesthetics of the Familiar: Everyday Life and World-Making*. Oxford: Oxford University Press, 2019.

Saito, Yuriko. *Everyday Aesthetics*. Oxford: Oxford University Press, 2007.

Scott, Geoffrey. *The Architecture of Humanism: A Study in the History of Taste*. New York City: Franklin Classics, 2018.

Scruton, Roger. *The Aesthetics of Architecture*. Princeton, N.J.: Princeton University Press, 2013.

Shaviro, Steven. *Discognition*. UK: Repeater, 2016.

Shelley, James. "The Default Theory of Aesthetic Value." *The British Journal of Aesthetics* 59, no. 1 (2018): 1–12.

Shubow, Justin. "Architecture Continues to Implode: More Insiders Admit the Profession Is Failing." *Forbes,* January 9, 2015: https://www.forbes.com/sites/justinshubow/2015/01/06/architecture-continues-to-implode-more-insiders-admit-the-profession-is-failing/?sh=663c8d094378.

United Nations. *Revision of World Urbanization Prospects Produced by the Population Division of the UN Department of Economic and Social Affairs (UN DESA)*. Current database. https://www.un.org/en/desa/2018-revision-world-urbanization-prospects#:~:text=The%202018%20Revision%20of%20World,in%20just%20a%20few%20countries.

Vasari, Giorgio, Betty Burroughs, and Jonathan Foster. *Vasari's Lives of the Artists: Biographies of the Most Eminent Architects, Painters, and Sculptors of Italy*. New York: Simon & Schuster, 1946.

Weitz, Morris. "The Role of Theory in Aesthetics." *Journal of Aesthetics and Art Criticism* 15, no. 1: 27–35.

Wilson, Alan T. "The Virtue of Aesthetic Courage." *British Journal of Aesthetics* 60, no. 4 (2020): 455–69.

Young, Michael. "Fear of the Mediated Image." *Cornell Journal of Architecture,* no. 11 (August 25, 2020): 146–61.

Zangwill, Nick. *Aesthetic Creation*. Oxford: Oxford University Press, 2012.

Zangwill, Nick. "In Defence of Moderate Aesthetic Formalism." *The Philosophical Quarterly (1950–)* 50, no. 201. (2000): 476–93.

Zangwill, Nick. *The Metaphysics of Beauty.* Ithaca, N.Y.: Cornell University Press, 2001.

Zeki, Semir. "Clive Bell's 'Significant Form' and the Neurobiology of Aesthetics." In *Frontiers in Human Neuroscience,* U.S. National Library of Medicine 7, Article 730 (November 12, 2013): 1–14.

(Continued from page iii)

Forerunners: Ideas First

Mark Foster Gage is principal of Mark Foster Gage Architects in New York City, Robert A. M. Stern Professor of Architecture at Yale University, founder of the Mark Foster Gage Foundation, and an accredited angel investor focusing on the artificial intelligence and virtual reality industries. He has published nine books, including *Architecture in High Resolution, Mark Foster Gage: Projects and Provocations, Aesthetics Equals Politics,* Speaking of Architecture, Aesthetic Theory: Essential Texts, and *Designing Social Equality: Architecture, Aesthetics, and the Perception of Democracy.*